ENDANGERED ANIMALS

A TRUE BOOK

by

Rhonda Lucas Donald

Children's Press®
A Division of Scholastic Inc.

New York Toronto London Auckland Sydney
Mexico City New Delhi Hong Kong
Danbury, Connecticut

A littered beach in Rio de Janeiro, Brazil.

Reading Consultant
Linda Cornwell
Coordinator of School Quality
and Professional Improvement
Indiana State
Teachers Association

Content Consultant
Jan Jenner
Rendalia Biologist
Talladega, AL

Author's Dedication:
For Samantha

Library of Congress Cataloging-in-Publication Data

Donald, Rhonda Lucas, 1962–
    Endangered animals / by Rhonda Lucas Donald.
        p. cm. — (A True book)
    Includes bibliographical references and index (p.)
    Summary: Examines the reasons why animals are threatened with
extinction and provides ways to help prevent their loss.
ISBN 0-516-22192-2 (lib. bdg.)   0-516-25999-7 (pbk.)
    1. Endangered species—Juvenile literature. [1. Endangered species.]
I. Title. II. Series.

    QL83.D68 2001   591.68—dc21
                                                             00-057043

Contents

Dinosaurs (above) became extinct around 65 million years ago. An asteroid like this (left) may have killed off the dinosaurs.

Extinction Is Forever

Dinosaurs are probably the most "famous" vanished animals. Some scientists believe they became extinct after a giant asteroid smashed into Earth sixty-five million years ago. Extinction is part of nature. Five times in history, though, there have been big extinctions in which many species, or kinds of plants and animals, like the dinosaurs, were wiped out. Natural events such as climatic changes or asteroid impacts caused these extinctions. The sixth extinction is taking place right now. But this one is quite different because it is being caused by people. Some experts warn that people are causing species to be wiped out hundreds of times faster than they should be.

In the movies, scientists can bring extinct animals such as dinosaurs back to life. In the real

A nature center graveyard for extinct animals (above). Millions of passenger pigeons (right) existed in the mid-1800s. By 1914, they were extinct and gone forever.

world, however, once an animal is gone, it is gone forever. The only thing we can do is to stop animals from becoming extinct in the first place.

Why Are Animals Vanishing

With a world population of more than six billion, people are taking over animals' homes (habitats). People cut down trees, fill in wetlands, clear land for crops or live-stock, dam rivers, build homes and businesses, and

Parking lot construction is one way habitats are destroyed (top). A housing development is taking over wetlands (bottom).

pollute the air and water.
When people change habitats,
many animals cannot survive in
them anymore. That is what
happened to the ivory-billed

A logger cuts down a tree (above). Ivory-billed woodpeckers (right).

woodpecker. It once lived in forests in the southern part of the United States. As loggers, miners, and builders cut the forests down, the woodpeckers

Animals like the strawberry poison-arrow frog (left) and the three-toed sloth (right) lose their homes when forest is cut or burned down (top).

died off, and they are now believed to be extinct in the United States. Thousands of other species lose their homes when people cut or burn down acres of rainforest every day.

People may also kill animals on purpose, helping to drive species to extinction. Among these people are those who prize wild cats as hunting trophies or for their beautiful fur. The tiger, elephant, and

Tigers (top), jaguars (bottom), rhinos (opposite left), and elephants (opposite right) are all hunted for profit.

rhinoceros face other kinds of problems. Traditional healers in the Far East use tiger bones and organs and rhino horns as health remedies. People seek

African elephants
(above) are illegally
hunted for their
ivory tusks (right).

elephants' ivory tusks to carve
into jewelry or decorative
pieces. Other hunters collect
sea turtles' eggs, meat, and

Green sea turtles face many threats. They are hunted, their nesting grounds are being destroyed, and they can drown in shrimp nets. Today, all species of sea turtles are in trouble.

shells. When animals become scarce, the money paid for their parts goes up, making it more profitable for someone to poach, or kill them illegally.

Gray wolf

Wolves: Victims of Fear

Before European settlers came to North America, wolves roamed most of the continent. However, Europeans brought their fear and hatred of wolves to the New World. They believed wolves were pests that preyed upon livestock and terrorized people. Moreover, the government paid money for dead wolves. By the 1930s there were few wolves left in the lower forty-eight states. Today, most people understand that wolves are not the bloodthirsty killers described in fairy tales. Gray wolves have been brought from Canada to live in Yellowstone National Park. Even though some people do not want the wolves there, most people are glad they are back. The wolves are thriving in their new home.

Introduced Aspen trees nearly wiped out Karner blue butterflies in New York. Shade from the trees kept lupines—the butterflies' natural food source—from growing.

Sometimes animals may cause trouble when people introduce them to a place where they have never been

Nene

before. This is especially true on islands. Hunting had already threatened Hawaii's nene (NAY-nay) goose, but livestock brought to the islands also destroyed the bird's nesting grounds. To make matters worse, people brought mongooses to help control rats. Instead, the mongooses preyed upon nene eggs. By 1947, there were only thirty nenes left. Scientists worked quickly to save the remaining birds. They brought the nenes to zoos and raised chicks that they then released back into the wild. The birds bounced back!

Ways of Helping

Raising rare animals in captivity is one way of saving endangered species. Not only nenes but also black-footed ferrets, California condors, golden lion tamarins, and whooping cranes have benefited from this kind of program. Some animals cannot live in captivity,

Black-footed ferrets (top), California condors (middle left), and golden lion tamarins (middle right) have all done well after being raised in captivity. A whooping crane in captivity (bottom) is kept clean.

though, or cannot be success-
fully released. Tigers and
other wild cats raised in captivity cannot be released
because they lack the hunting
skills they need to survive.
Only mother cats in the wild
can teach their cubs these
skills.

　　Saving endangered animals
is mostly about saving the
wild places where they live.
Desert tortoises have lost
their habitat to development

A desert tortoise (above). A sign on a fence at a Desert Tortoise Natural Area (right).

Desert Tortoise
NATURAL AREA

THE AREA BEHIND SIGN

CLOSED
TO ALL VEHICLE USE

TO PROTECT NATURAL VALUES

and even face danger from drivers of off-road vehicles who ride through their territory, sometimes burying the tortoises' burrows. To help the tortoises, scientists came up with a Species Survival Plan that protects the tortoises' habitat. Building is restricted, and so is access to those riding off road. Anyone caught harming a protected species faces stiff punishment.

Cleaning up our planet helps all living things, including endangered animals. When birds of prey were dying off, only a ban on the pesticide DDT could save them. The pesticide caused the birds' eggs to be brittle and break before they hatched. Now that DDT is illegal in the United States, many of the birds have recovered. Restoring habitats is also important. Several years ago some people who wanted to build homes and businesses in Florida filled in the Everglades and changed the natural flow of water, putting many species in danger. Conservation and government groups have

Florida Everglades

The snail kite (top), Florida panther (middle left), American crocodile (middle right), and manatee (bottom) are just a few endangered Everglades animals.

come up with a plan to restore the Everglades by building man-made wetlands, removing dams, and cleaning up polluted water.

The best-known help in protecting endangered animals is the Endangered Species Act. This law protects animals by putting them on a list. Endangered species on the list are so rare that they face extinction if people do nothing to help them. The law also lists threatened species that can become endangered if they are not helped. Blue whales, tigers, gray bats, and whooping cranes are endangered. Threatened animals include the desert tortoise, Canada lynx, and northern spotted owl. Once an animal is on the list, the government can do things to protect it and its habitat—as in the case of the desert tortoise.

Animals like the gray bat (left), lynx (middle left), northern spotted owl (middle right), tiger (bottom left), and blue whale (bottom right) need protection.

At Home

Prairie dog burrows are also home to insects, spiders, snakes, rodents, burrowing owls, and the highly endangered black-footed ferret. The dogs' digging helps mix up the soil, and their droppings enrich it, helping plants to grow better. Prairie dogs keep the grasses

Where do these animals fit into a prairie dog town?

near their burrows trimmed short, which makes the grass shoots more nutritious for grazing animals such as bison.

Poisoning of prairie dogs, which many ranchers consider pests, led to the near extinction of black-footed ferrets. Now the ferrets are doing better thanks to captive breeding and release programs. But sadly, prairie dogs are now threatened, having lost nearly all their habitat to farming and ranching. If prairie dogs vanished from this ecosystem, what might happen to the other animals and plants that depend on them?

Many animals share the prairie dog's habitat.

Why Save Animals?

Can you imagine living in a world where the only place you could see wild animals was in a zoo? Sounds like a sad place. The extinction that is taking place now will not wipe out all the animals, but it will harm the biodiversity, or many different kinds,

There may be more tigers living in captivity than in the wild.

of life on Earth. Places with a large variety of plants and animals are healthy ecosystems, or communities of life. Each animal in an ecosystem has an important part to play. When all the parts are in place, the ecosystem works well. When a part is missing, however, as when an animal becomes extinct, the system may break down. If the world's ecosystems are not healthy, people will suffer too because we depend on the variety of life on Earth.

Not everyone agrees that it is important to help endangered animals. Some people believe that animals' needs are not as important as people's needs. In contrast, others believe that the world would be a much poorer place without the many different animals that share the Earth. The truth is, we do not know what might happen if many species become extinct. We could lose more than just the animals. If you want to help animals and the wild places where they live, here are some ways:

• Conserve energy and resources such as water and paper. Recycle what you can, and try to create as little waste as possible.

• Avoid using pesticides or other toxic chemicals both indoors and out.

• Never litter—trash can harm animals.

A seagull is caught in a plastic six-pack ring.

Students recycle live Christmas trees by planting them on school property.

• Create habitats by planting trees, shrubs, and flowers. Turn your yard or school grounds into a place where animals can live.

• Get involved. Students at Dover Shores Elementary in Orlando, Florida, held a Manatee Mart. The kids made bookmarks, puzzles, and other manatee goodies to sell. They raised and donated hundreds of dollars to help protect manatees and to teach others about these endangered animals.

To Find Out More

To learn more about endangered animals, check out these resources:

 **Books**

Charman, Andy. **I Wonder Why the Dodo Is Dead and Other Questions About Extinct and Endangered Animals.** Kingfisher Books, 1996.

Facklam, Margery. **And Then There Was One: The Mysteries of Extinction.** Little Brown, 1993.

Few, Roger and Laurence Pringle. **MacMillan Children's Guide to Endangered Animals.** Simon and Schuster, 1993.

Kest, Kristin. **Endangered Animals: 140 Species in Full Color.** Golden Books, 1995.

Organizations and Online Sites

American Museum of Natural History
175-208 Central Park West
New York, NY 10024
(212) 769-5100
http://www.amnh.org/Exhibition/Expedition/Endangered

This site is a virtual tour of an exhibit at the museum. It features an overview of endangered animals, and it highlights thirty-four animals with photos, maps, and lots of information.

U.S. Fish and Wildlife Service Department of the Interior
1849 C St., NW
Washington, DC 20240
http://www.fws.gov/kids

This is the government agency responsible for protecting threatened and endangered species. You can find information about all the listed species along with games and lots of ways to help.

U.S. Geological Survey
http://biology.usgs.gov/features/kidscorner/kidscrnr.html

This organization offers an online coloring book featuring twenty different endangered plants and animals that you can print out and color.

World Wildlife Fund
1250 24th St., NW
Washington, DC
20037-1175
(202) 293-4800
http://www.wwfus.org

This organization works to protect animals all over the world. The site has games, quizzes, activities, fact sheets, and a photo gallery of endangered species.

Important Words

biodiversity the many different kinds of life on Earth

ecosystem the living and nonliving things that depend on one another in a habitat

endangered species a plant or animal that is so rare that it may become extinct if people do nothing to help

Endangered Species Act a law passed in 1973 that protects threatened and endangered species in the United States

habitat a place where living things find food, water, shelter, and others of their kind

introduced species a plant or animal brought by people to an area where it has never existed before

poach to kill a protected animal illegally

threatened species a species that can become endangered if people do not prevent it

Index

Meet the Author

Rhonda Lucas Donald has written for children and teachers for fifteen years. Her work has appeared in magazines such as *Ranger Rick* and *Your Big Backyard*. She specializes in writing about science and natural history and creating projects that make these subjects fun. Rhonda received the EdPress award for best newsletter of 1997 for *EarthSavers*, an environmental newspaper and activity guide. She has also written several other environmental True Books for Children's Press. She lives in North Carolina with her husband Bruce, cats Sophie and Tory, and Maggie the dog.